Take a Guess:
A Look At Estimation

by Janine Scott

Content and Reading Adviser: Mary Beth Fletcher, Ed.D.
Educational Consultant/Reading Specialist
The Carroll School, Lincoln, Massachusetts

Spyglass
BOOKS

COMPASS POINT BOOKS

Minneapolis, Minnesota

Compass Point Books
3109 West 50th Street, #115
Minneapolis, MN 55410

Visit Compass Point Books on the Internet at *www.compasspointbooks.com*
or e-mail your request to *custserv@compasspointbooks.com*

Photographs ©: RubberBall Productions, cover; Bob Krist/Corbis, 4; Digital Vision, 5; Ariel
Skelley/Corbis, 6; Phil Bulgasch, 7, 9, 14; PhotoDisc, 8, 10; Jose Luis Pelaez, Inc./Corbis, 11, 19; Index
Stock Imagery/Dennis Curran, 12; Unicorn Stock Photos/Jim Shippee, 13; Kevin Fleming/Corbis, 15;
Roger Ressmeyer/Corbis, 16; Owen Franken/Corbis, 17; Tom Stewart/Corbis, 18.

Project Manager: Rebecca Weber McEwen
Editors: Heidi Schoof and Patricia Stockland
Photo Researcher: Svetlana Zhurkina
Designer: Jaime Martens
Illustrator: Anna-Maria Crum

Library of Congress Cataloging-in-Publication Data
Scott, Janine.
  Take a guess / by Janine Scott.
    p. cm. — (Spyglass books)
Summary: Presents the concept of estimation and how important it can be
to give an approximate measure, such as when adding a pinch of salt to a
recipe or rounding off one's age.
Includes bibliographical references and index.
  ISBN 0-7565-0446-5 (hardcover)
  1. Estimation theory—Juvenile literature. [1. Estimation theory.]
  I. Title. II. Series.
  QA276.8 .S26 2003
  519.5'44—dc21   2002012622

Contents

NOTE: Glossary words are in **bold** the first time they appear.

Take a Guess

Every day, people measure things. Sometimes they use measuring tools. Sometimes they don't.

You can often tell if someone is taller than another person just by looking.

What Weighs More?

You can guess how much something weighs. Usually, something big weighs more than something small.

Sometimes, something small weighs more than something big.

What Holds More?

You can guess how much something can hold. Something with a big space holds more than something with a little space.

These glasses have different shapes. Which will hold more? 9

What Time Is It?

You can guess what time it is.
When the sun is high in the sky, it is close to noon.

When our stomachs *growl,*
it is time for dinner.

11

Wet or Dry?

You can guess what
the weather is like.
When you look outside,
you can tell if it is sunny
or cloudy, wet or dry.

Weather forecasters guess, too. They have a good idea of what weather might happen, but they don't know for sure.

How Many People?

You can guess how many people are voting. Sometimes people say their votes out loud. The loudest group wins the vote.

Sometimes people write down their votes when an *exact* count is needed.

Cooking Count

You can guess how much food to add when cooking. Many cooks do not measure. They know how much to put in just by looking at the food.

Recipes use words that help a cook take a guess. How much is a "dash" of pepper? How much is a "pinch" of salt?

Close Enough

You can guess many different things.
Many people can guess how much they weigh, even if they don't know the exact number.

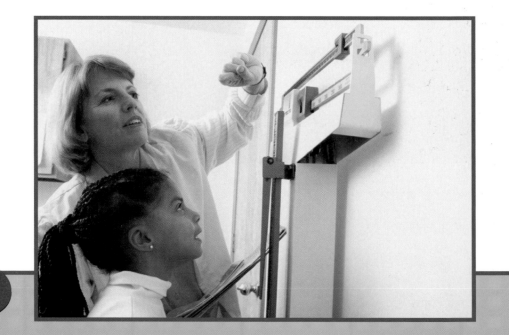

You do not always need to be exact. You can say it is three o'clock, even if it is a few minutes before or after three.

Fun Facts

How Old?
You can tell how old a horse is by looking at its teeth! The older a horse gets, the longer and sharper its teeth get.

How Long?
Scientists study volcanoes so they can try to guess when the volcanoes might *erupt* next.

How Heavy?

A whale is too big for a scale.
Scientists can guess how many
tons a whale might weigh by
looking at
how long
it is.

How Many?

People who work at a bakery
need to guess how many *customers*
they might have each day. This
way, they can make sure they
have made enough food to sell.

Glossary

customers–people who buy things from a store

erupt–when a volcano throws out rocks, hot ashes, and lava with great force

exact–perfectly correct

growl–to make a low, deep noise like an angry animal

recipe–instructions for preparing and cooking food

ton–2,000 pounds

weather forecaster–a person who tells what the weather will be like for the next day or the next few days

Learn More

Books

Dinio-Durkin, Cecilia. *Hickory Dickory Math: Teaching Math with Nursery Rhymes and Fairy Tales.* New York: Scholastic Press, 1997.

Murphy, Stuart J. *Betcha!: Estimating (MathStart).* New York, NY: HarperCollins Publishers, 1997.

Tang, Greg. *Math for All Seasons.* New York: Scholastic Press, 2002.

Web Sites

Math Cats
www.mathcats.com/microworlds/
whatacrowd.html

PBS Kids
http://pbskids.org/cyberchase/classroom/
lesson2handout.pdf

Index

GR: H
Word Count: 164

From Janine Scott

I live in New Zealand and have two daughters. They love to read books that are full of fun facts and features. I hope you do, too!

24